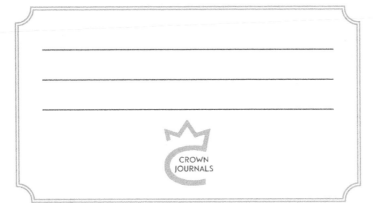

CROWN
JOURNALS

Reunion Guest Book

NAME:

BIRTHDAY: | ANNIVERSARY:

ADDRESS:

CONTACT NUMBER: | MOBILE NUMBER:

EMAIL:

CHILDREN & BIRTHDAYS:

FAVORITE MEMORY:

NAME:

BIRTHDAY: | ANNIVERSARY:

ADDRESS:

CONTACT NUMBER: | MOBILE NUMBER:

EMAIL:

CHILDREN & BIRTHDAYS:

FAVORITE MEMORY:

Reunion Guest Book

NAME:

BIRTHDAY: ANNIVERSARY:

ADDRESS:

CONTACT NUMBER: MOBILE NUMBER:

EMAIL:

CHILDREN & BIRTHDAYS:

FAVORITE MEMORY:

NAME:

BIRTHDAY: ANNIVERSARY:

ADDRESS:

CONTACT NUMBER: MOBILE NUMBER:

EMAIL:

CHILDREN & BIRTHDAYS:

FAVORITE MEMORY:

Reunion Guest Book

NAME:

BIRTHDAY: | ANNIVERSARY:

ADDRESS:

CONTACT NUMBER: | MOBILE NUMBER:

EMAIL:

CHILDREN & BIRTHDAYS:

FAVORITE MEMORY:

NAME:

BIRTHDAY: | ANNIVERSARY:

ADDRESS:

CONTACT NUMBER: | MOBILE NUMBER:

EMAIL:

CHILDREN & BIRTHDAYS:

FAVORITE MEMORY:

Reunion Guest Book

NAME:

BIRTHDAY: ANNIVERSARY:

ADDRESS: —————————————————————

CONTACT NUMBER: MOBILE NUMBER:

EMAIL:

CHILDREN & BIRTHDAYS:

FAVORITE MEMORY:

NAME:

BIRTHDAY: ANNIVERSARY:

ADDRESS: —————————————————————

CONTACT NUMBER: MOBILE NUMBER:

EMAIL:

CHILDREN & BIRTHDAYS:

FAVORITE MEMORY:

Reunion Guest Book

NAME:

BIRTHDAY: ANNIVERSARY:

ADDRESS: ———————————————————

CONTACT NUMBER: MOBILE NUMBER:

EMAIL:

CHILDREN & BIRTHDAYS:

FAVORITE MEMORY:

NAME:

BIRTHDAY: ANNIVERSARY:

ADDRESS: ———————————————————

CONTACT NUMBER: MOBILE NUMBER:

EMAIL:

CHILDREN & BIRTHDAYS:

FAVORITE MEMORY:

Reunion Guest Book

NAME:

BIRTHDAY: ANNIVERSARY:

ADDRESS: ——————————————

CONTACT NUMBER: MOBILE NUMBER:

EMAIL:

CHILDREN & BIRTHDAYS:

FAVORITE MEMORY:

NAME:

BIRTHDAY: ANNIVERSARY:

ADDRESS: ——————————————

CONTACT NUMBER: MOBILE NUMBER:

EMAIL:

CHILDREN & BIRTHDAYS:

FAVORITE MEMORY:

Reunion Guest Book

NAME:

BIRTHDAY: | ANNIVERSARY:

ADDRESS: ——————————————

CONTACT NUMBER: | MOBILE NUMBER:

EMAIL:

CHILDREN & BIRTHDAYS:

FAVORITE MEMORY:

NAME:

BIRTHDAY: | ANNIVERSARY:

ADDRESS: ——————————————

CONTACT NUMBER: | MOBILE NUMBER:

EMAIL:

CHILDREN & BIRTHDAYS:

FAVORITE MEMORY:

Reunion Guest Book

NAME:

BIRTHDAY: | ANNIVERSARY:

ADDRESS: ——————————————————

CONTACT NUMBER: | MOBILE NUMBER:

EMAIL:

CHILDREN & BIRTHDAYS:

FAVORITE MEMORY:

NAME:

BIRTHDAY: | ANNIVERSARY:

ADDRESS: ——————————————————

CONTACT NUMBER: | MOBILE NUMBER:

EMAIL:

CHILDREN & BIRTHDAYS:

FAVORITE MEMORY:

Reunion Guest Book

NAME:

BIRTHDAY: | ANNIVERSARY:

ADDRESS:

CONTACT NUMBER: | MOBILE NUMBER:

EMAIL:

CHILDREN & BIRTHDAYS:

FAVORITE MEMORY:

NAME:

BIRTHDAY: | ANNIVERSARY:

ADDRESS:

CONTACT NUMBER: | MOBILE NUMBER:

EMAIL:

CHILDREN & BIRTHDAYS:

FAVORITE MEMORY:

Reunion Guest Book

NAME:

BIRTHDAY: | ANNIVERSARY:

ADDRESS:

CONTACT NUMBER: | MOBILE NUMBER:

EMAIL:

CHILDREN & BIRTHDAYS:

FAVORITE MEMORY:

NAME:

BIRTHDAY: | ANNIVERSARY:

ADDRESS:

CONTACT NUMBER: | MOBILE NUMBER:

EMAIL:

CHILDREN & BIRTHDAYS:

FAVORITE MEMORY:

Reunion Guest Book

NAME:

BIRTHDAY: | ANNIVERSARY:

ADDRESS: ――――――――――

CONTACT NUMBER: | MOBILE NUMBER:

EMAIL:

CHILDREN & BIRTHDAYS:

FAVORITE MEMORY:

NAME:

BIRTHDAY: | ANNIVERSARY:

ADDRESS: ――――――――――

CONTACT NUMBER: | MOBILE NUMBER:

EMAIL:

CHILDREN & BIRTHDAYS:

FAVORITE MEMORY:

Reunion Guest Book

NAME:

BIRTHDAY: ANNIVERSARY:

ADDRESS: —————————————————————

CONTACT NUMBER: MOBILE NUMBER:

EMAIL:

CHILDREN & BIRTHDAYS:

FAVORITE MEMORY:

NAME:

BIRTHDAY: ANNIVERSARY:

ADDRESS: —————————————————————

CONTACT NUMBER: MOBILE NUMBER:

EMAIL:

CHILDREN & BIRTHDAYS:

FAVORITE MEMORY:

Reunion Guest Book

NAME:

BIRTHDAY: ANNIVERSARY:

ADDRESS: ————

CONTACT NUMBER: MOBILE NUMBER:

EMAIL:

CHILDREN & BIRTHDAYS:

FAVORITE MEMORY:

NAME:

BIRTHDAY: ANNIVERSARY:

ADDRESS: ————

CONTACT NUMBER: MOBILE NUMBER:

EMAIL:

CHILDREN & BIRTHDAYS:

FAVORITE MEMORY:

Reunion Guest Book

NAME:

BIRTHDAY: | ANNIVERSARY:

ADDRESS: ————————————————————————————————

CONTACT NUMBER: | MOBILE NUMBER:

EMAIL:

CHILDREN & BIRTHDAYS:

FAVORITE MEMORY:

NAME:

BIRTHDAY: | ANNIVERSARY:

ADDRESS: ————————————————————————————————

CONTACT NUMBER: | MOBILE NUMBER:

EMAIL:

CHILDREN & BIRTHDAYS:

FAVORITE MEMORY:

Reunion Guest Book

NAME:

BIRTHDAY: | ANNIVERSARY:

ADDRESS:

CONTACT NUMBER: | MOBILE NUMBER:

EMAIL:

CHILDREN & BIRTHDAYS:

FAVORITE MEMORY:

NAME:

BIRTHDAY: | ANNIVERSARY:

ADDRESS:

CONTACT NUMBER: | MOBILE NUMBER:

EMAIL:

CHILDREN & BIRTHDAYS:

FAVORITE MEMORY:

Reunion Guest Book

NAME:

BIRTHDAY: ANNIVERSARY:

ADDRESS:

CONTACT NUMBER: MOBILE NUMBER:

EMAIL:

CHILDREN & BIRTHDAYS:

FAVORITE MEMORY:

NAME:

BIRTHDAY: ANNIVERSARY:

ADDRESS:

CONTACT NUMBER: MOBILE NUMBER:

EMAIL:

CHILDREN & BIRTHDAYS:

FAVORITE MEMORY:

Reunion Guest Book

NAME:

BIRTHDAY: | ANNIVERSARY:

ADDRESS:

CONTACT NUMBER: | MOBILE NUMBER:

EMAIL:

CHILDREN & BIRTHDAYS:

FAVORITE MEMORY:

NAME:

BIRTHDAY: | ANNIVERSARY:

ADDRESS:

CONTACT NUMBER: | MOBILE NUMBER:

EMAIL:

CHILDREN & BIRTHDAYS:

FAVORITE MEMORY:

Reunion Guest Book

NAME:

BIRTHDAY: | ANNIVERSARY:

ADDRESS: ————————————————

CONTACT NUMBER: | MOBILE NUMBER:

EMAIL:

CHILDREN & BIRTHDAYS:

FAVORITE MEMORY:

NAME:

BIRTHDAY: | ANNIVERSARY:

ADDRESS: ————————————————

CONTACT NUMBER: | MOBILE NUMBER:

EMAIL:

CHILDREN & BIRTHDAYS:

FAVORITE MEMORY:

Reunion Guest Book

NAME:

BIRTHDAY: ANNIVERSARY:

ADDRESS:

CONTACT NUMBER: MOBILE NUMBER:

EMAIL:

CHILDREN & BIRTHDAYS:

FAVORITE MEMORY:

NAME:

BIRTHDAY: ANNIVERSARY:

ADDRESS:

CONTACT NUMBER: MOBILE NUMBER:

EMAIL:

CHILDREN & BIRTHDAYS:

FAVORITE MEMORY:

Reunion Guest Book

NAME:

BIRTHDAY: ANNIVERSARY:

ADDRESS: ——————————————————————

CONTACT NUMBER: MOBILE NUMBER:

EMAIL:

CHILDREN & BIRTHDAYS:

FAVORITE MEMORY:

NAME:

BIRTHDAY: ANNIVERSARY:

ADDRESS: ——————————————————————

CONTACT NUMBER: MOBILE NUMBER:

EMAIL:

CHILDREN & BIRTHDAYS:

FAVORITE MEMORY:

Reunion Guest Book

NAME:

BIRTHDAY:

ANNIVERSARY:

ADDRESS:

CONTACT NUMBER:

MOBILE NUMBER:

EMAIL:

CHILDREN & BIRTHDAYS:

FAVORITE MEMORY:

NAME:

BIRTHDAY:

ANNIVERSARY:

ADDRESS:

CONTACT NUMBER:

MOBILE NUMBER:

EMAIL:

CHILDREN & BIRTHDAYS:

FAVORITE MEMORY:

Reunion Guest Book

NAME:

BIRTHDAY: | ANNIVERSARY:

ADDRESS: ———————————————————————

CONTACT NUMBER: | MOBILE NUMBER:

EMAIL:

CHILDREN & BIRTHDAYS:

FAVORITE MEMORY:

NAME:

BIRTHDAY: | ANNIVERSARY:

ADDRESS: ———————————————————————

CONTACT NUMBER: | MOBILE NUMBER:

EMAIL:

CHILDREN & BIRTHDAYS:

FAVORITE MEMORY:

Reunion Guest Book

NAME:

BIRTHDAY: | ANNIVERSARY:

ADDRESS:

CONTACT NUMBER: | MOBILE NUMBER:

EMAIL:

CHILDREN & BIRTHDAYS:

FAVORITE MEMORY:

NAME:

BIRTHDAY: | ANNIVERSARY:

ADDRESS:

CONTACT NUMBER: | MOBILE NUMBER:

EMAIL:

CHILDREN & BIRTHDAYS:

FAVORITE MEMORY:

Reunion Guest Book

NAME:

BIRTHDAY: | ANNIVERSARY:

ADDRESS:

CONTACT NUMBER: | MOBILE NUMBER:

EMAIL:

CHILDREN & BIRTHDAYS:

FAVORITE MEMORY:

NAME:

BIRTHDAY: | ANNIVERSARY:

ADDRESS:

CONTACT NUMBER: | MOBILE NUMBER:

EMAIL:

CHILDREN & BIRTHDAYS:

FAVORITE MEMORY:

Reunion Guest Book

NAME:

BIRTHDAY: | ANNIVERSARY:

ADDRESS: —————————————

CONTACT NUMBER: | MOBILE NUMBER:

EMAIL:

CHILDREN & BIRTHDAYS:

FAVORITE MEMORY:

NAME:

BIRTHDAY: | ANNIVERSARY:

ADDRESS: —————————————

CONTACT NUMBER: | MOBILE NUMBER:

EMAIL:

CHILDREN & BIRTHDAYS:

FAVORITE MEMORY:

Reunion Guest Book

NAME:

BIRTHDAY: | ANNIVERSARY:

ADDRESS: ——————————————

CONTACT NUMBER: | MOBILE NUMBER:

EMAIL:

CHILDREN & BIRTHDAYS:

FAVORITE MEMORY:

NAME:

BIRTHDAY: | ANNIVERSARY:

ADDRESS: ——————————————

CONTACT NUMBER: | MOBILE NUMBER:

EMAIL:

CHILDREN & BIRTHDAYS:

FAVORITE MEMORY:

Reunion Guest Book

NAME:

BIRTHDAY: | ANNIVERSARY:

ADDRESS: ——————————————

CONTACT NUMBER: | MOBILE NUMBER:

EMAIL:

CHILDREN & BIRTHDAYS:

FAVORITE MEMORY:

NAME:

BIRTHDAY: | ANNIVERSARY:

ADDRESS: ——————————————

CONTACT NUMBER: | MOBILE NUMBER:

EMAIL:

CHILDREN & BIRTHDAYS:

FAVORITE MEMORY:

Reunion Guest Book

NAME:

BIRTHDAY:

ANNIVERSARY:

ADDRESS:

CONTACT NUMBER:

MOBILE NUMBER:

EMAIL:

CHILDREN & BIRTHDAYS:

FAVORITE MEMORY:

NAME:

BIRTHDAY:

ANNIVERSARY:

ADDRESS:

CONTACT NUMBER:

MOBILE NUMBER:

EMAIL:

CHILDREN & BIRTHDAYS:

FAVORITE MEMORY:

Reunion Guest Book

NAME:

BIRTHDAY: | ANNIVERSARY:

ADDRESS: —————————————————

CONTACT NUMBER: | MOBILE NUMBER:

EMAIL:

CHILDREN & BIRTHDAYS:

FAVORITE MEMORY:

NAME:

BIRTHDAY: | ANNIVERSARY:

ADDRESS: —————————————————

CONTACT NUMBER: | MOBILE NUMBER:

EMAIL:

CHILDREN & BIRTHDAYS:

FAVORITE MEMORY:

Reunion Guest Book

NAME:

BIRTHDAY: | ANNIVERSARY:

ADDRESS: ————————————————

CONTACT NUMBER: | MOBILE NUMBER:

EMAIL:

CHILDREN & BIRTHDAYS:

FAVORITE MEMORY:

NAME:

BIRTHDAY: | ANNIVERSARY:

ADDRESS: ————————————————

CONTACT NUMBER: | MOBILE NUMBER:

EMAIL:

CHILDREN & BIRTHDAYS:

FAVORITE MEMORY:

Reunion Guest Book

NAME:

BIRTHDAY: | ANNIVERSARY:

ADDRESS:

CONTACT NUMBER: | MOBILE NUMBER:

EMAIL:

CHILDREN & BIRTHDAYS:

FAVORITE MEMORY:

NAME:

BIRTHDAY: | ANNIVERSARY:

ADDRESS:

CONTACT NUMBER: | MOBILE NUMBER:

EMAIL:

CHILDREN & BIRTHDAYS:

FAVORITE MEMORY:

Reunion Guest Book

NAME:

BIRTHDAY: | ANNIVERSARY:

ADDRESS:

CONTACT NUMBER: | MOBILE NUMBER:

EMAIL:

CHILDREN & BIRTHDAYS:

FAVORITE MEMORY:

NAME:

BIRTHDAY: | ANNIVERSARY:

ADDRESS:

CONTACT NUMBER: | MOBILE NUMBER:

EMAIL:

CHILDREN & BIRTHDAYS:

FAVORITE MEMORY:

Reunion Guest Book

NAME:

BIRTHDAY:

ANNIVERSARY:

ADDRESS: —————————————

CONTACT NUMBER:

MOBILE NUMBER:

EMAIL:

CHILDREN & BIRTHDAYS:

FAVORITE MEMORY:

NAME:

BIRTHDAY:

ANNIVERSARY:

ADDRESS: —————————————

CONTACT NUMBER:

MOBILE NUMBER:

EMAIL:

CHILDREN & BIRTHDAYS:

FAVORITE MEMORY:

Reunion Guest Book

NAME:

BIRTHDAY:	ANNIVERSARY:

ADDRESS: —————————————————————————

CONTACT NUMBER:	MOBILE NUMBER:

EMAIL:

CHILDREN & BIRTHDAYS:

FAVORITE MEMORY:

NAME:

BIRTHDAY:	ANNIVERSARY:

ADDRESS: —————————————————————————

CONTACT NUMBER:	MOBILE NUMBER:

EMAIL:

CHILDREN & BIRTHDAYS:

FAVORITE MEMORY:

Reunion Guest Book

NAME:

BIRTHDAY:	ANNIVERSARY:

ADDRESS: —————————————

CONTACT NUMBER:	MOBILE NUMBER:

EMAIL:

CHILDREN & BIRTHDAYS:

FAVORITE MEMORY:

NAME:

BIRTHDAY:	ANNIVERSARY:

ADDRESS: —————————————

CONTACT NUMBER:	MOBILE NUMBER:

EMAIL:

CHILDREN & BIRTHDAYS:

FAVORITE MEMORY:

Reunion Guest Book

NAME:

BIRTHDAY: | ANNIVERSARY:

ADDRESS: —————————————————

CONTACT NUMBER: | MOBILE NUMBER:

EMAIL:

CHILDREN & BIRTHDAYS:

FAVORITE MEMORY:

NAME:

BIRTHDAY: | ANNIVERSARY:

ADDRESS: —————————————————

CONTACT NUMBER: | MOBILE NUMBER:

EMAIL:

CHILDREN & BIRTHDAYS:

FAVORITE MEMORY:

Reunion Guest Book

NAME:

BIRTHDAY: | ANNIVERSARY:

ADDRESS:

CONTACT NUMBER: | MOBILE NUMBER:

EMAIL:

CHILDREN & BIRTHDAYS:

FAVORITE MEMORY:

NAME:

BIRTHDAY: | ANNIVERSARY:

ADDRESS:

CONTACT NUMBER: | MOBILE NUMBER:

EMAIL:

CHILDREN & BIRTHDAYS:

FAVORITE MEMORY:

Reunion Guest Book

NAME:

BIRTHDAY: | ANNIVERSARY:

ADDRESS: ————————————————

CONTACT NUMBER: | MOBILE NUMBER:

EMAIL:

CHILDREN & BIRTHDAYS:

FAVORITE MEMORY:

NAME:

BIRTHDAY: | ANNIVERSARY:

ADDRESS: ————————————————

CONTACT NUMBER: | MOBILE NUMBER:

EMAIL:

CHILDREN & BIRTHDAYS:

FAVORITE MEMORY:

Reunion Guest Book

NAME:

BIRTHDAY: | **ANNIVERSARY:**

ADDRESS: ———————————————

CONTACT NUMBER: | **MOBILE NUMBER:**

EMAIL:

CHILDREN & BIRTHDAYS:

FAVORITE MEMORY:

NAME:

BIRTHDAY: | **ANNIVERSARY:**

ADDRESS: ———————————————

CONTACT NUMBER: | **MOBILE NUMBER:**

EMAIL:

CHILDREN & BIRTHDAYS:

FAVORITE MEMORY:

Reunion Guest Book

NAME:

BIRTHDAY: | ANNIVERSARY:

ADDRESS: ———————————————

CONTACT NUMBER: | MOBILE NUMBER:

EMAIL:

CHILDREN & BIRTHDAYS:

FAVORITE MEMORY:

NAME:

BIRTHDAY: | ANNIVERSARY:

ADDRESS: ———————————————

CONTACT NUMBER: | MOBILE NUMBER:

EMAIL:

CHILDREN & BIRTHDAYS:

FAVORITE MEMORY:

Reunion Guest Book

NAME:

BIRTHDAY: | ANNIVERSARY:

ADDRESS:

CONTACT NUMBER: | MOBILE NUMBER:

EMAIL:

CHILDREN & BIRTHDAYS:

FAVORITE MEMORY:

NAME:

BIRTHDAY: | ANNIVERSARY:

ADDRESS:

CONTACT NUMBER: | MOBILE NUMBER:

EMAIL:

CHILDREN & BIRTHDAYS:

FAVORITE MEMORY:

Reunion Guest Book

NAME:

BIRTHDAY: | ANNIVERSARY:

ADDRESS: —————————————————————————

CONTACT NUMBER: | MOBILE NUMBER:

EMAIL:

CHILDREN & BIRTHDAYS:

FAVORITE MEMORY:

NAME:

BIRTHDAY: | ANNIVERSARY:

ADDRESS: —————————————————————————

CONTACT NUMBER: | MOBILE NUMBER:

EMAIL:

CHILDREN & BIRTHDAYS:

FAVORITE MEMORY:

Reunion Guest Book

NAME:

BIRTHDAY: | ANNIVERSARY:

ADDRESS: ―――――――――――――――

CONTACT NUMBER: | MOBILE NUMBER:

EMAIL:

CHILDREN & BIRTHDAYS:

FAVORITE MEMORY:

NAME:

BIRTHDAY: | ANNIVERSARY:

ADDRESS: ―――――――――――――――

CONTACT NUMBER: | MOBILE NUMBER:

EMAIL:

CHILDREN & BIRTHDAYS:

FAVORITE MEMORY:

Reunion Guest Book

NAME:

BIRTHDAY: | ANNIVERSARY:

ADDRESS: ————————————————————

CONTACT NUMBER: | MOBILE NUMBER:

EMAIL:

CHILDREN & BIRTHDAYS:

FAVORITE MEMORY:

NAME:

BIRTHDAY: | ANNIVERSARY:

ADDRESS: ————————————————————

CONTACT NUMBER: | MOBILE NUMBER:

EMAIL:

CHILDREN & BIRTHDAYS:

FAVORITE MEMORY:

Reunion Guest Book

NAME:

BIRTHDAY:

ANNIVERSARY:

ADDRESS:

CONTACT NUMBER:

MOBILE NUMBER:

EMAIL:

CHILDREN & BIRTHDAYS:

FAVORITE MEMORY:

NAME:

BIRTHDAY:

ANNIVERSARY:

ADDRESS:

CONTACT NUMBER:

MOBILE NUMBER:

EMAIL:

CHILDREN & BIRTHDAYS:

FAVORITE MEMORY:

Reunion Guest Book

NAME:

BIRTHDAY: | ANNIVERSARY:

ADDRESS: —————————————————————

CONTACT NUMBER: | MOBILE NUMBER:

EMAIL:

CHILDREN & BIRTHDAYS:

FAVORITE MEMORY:

NAME:

BIRTHDAY: | ANNIVERSARY:

ADDRESS: —————————————————————

CONTACT NUMBER: | MOBILE NUMBER:

EMAIL:

CHILDREN & BIRTHDAYS:

FAVORITE MEMORY:

Reunion Guest Book

NAME:

BIRTHDAY:	ANNIVERSARY:

ADDRESS: ——————————————

CONTACT NUMBER:	MOBILE NUMBER:

EMAIL:

CHILDREN & BIRTHDAYS:

FAVORITE MEMORY:

NAME:

BIRTHDAY:	ANNIVERSARY:

ADDRESS: ——————————————

CONTACT NUMBER:	MOBILE NUMBER:

EMAIL:

CHILDREN & BIRTHDAYS:

FAVORITE MEMORY:

Reunion Guest Book

NAME:

BIRTHDAY: ANNIVERSARY:

ADDRESS: ————————

CONTACT NUMBER: MOBILE NUMBER:

EMAIL:

CHILDREN & BIRTHDAYS:

FAVORITE MEMORY:

NAME:

BIRTHDAY: ANNIVERSARY:

ADDRESS: ————————

CONTACT NUMBER: MOBILE NUMBER:

EMAIL:

CHILDREN & BIRTHDAYS:

FAVORITE MEMORY:

Reunion Guest Book

NAME:

BIRTHDAY: ANNIVERSARY:

ADDRESS:

CONTACT NUMBER: MOBILE NUMBER:

EMAIL:

CHILDREN & BIRTHDAYS:

FAVORITE MEMORY:

NAME:

BIRTHDAY: ANNIVERSARY:

ADDRESS:

CONTACT NUMBER: MOBILE NUMBER:

EMAIL:

CHILDREN & BIRTHDAYS:

FAVORITE MEMORY:

Reunion Guest Book

NAME:

BIRTHDAY: | ANNIVERSARY:

ADDRESS: —————————

CONTACT NUMBER: | MOBILE NUMBER:

EMAIL:

CHILDREN & BIRTHDAYS:

FAVORITE MEMORY:

NAME:

BIRTHDAY: | ANNIVERSARY:

ADDRESS: —————————

CONTACT NUMBER: | MOBILE NUMBER:

EMAIL:

CHILDREN & BIRTHDAYS:

FAVORITE MEMORY:

Reunion Guest Book

NAME:

BIRTHDAY: | ANNIVERSARY:

ADDRESS:

CONTACT NUMBER: | MOBILE NUMBER:

EMAIL:

CHILDREN & BIRTHDAYS:

FAVORITE MEMORY:

NAME:

BIRTHDAY: | ANNIVERSARY:

ADDRESS:

CONTACT NUMBER: | MOBILE NUMBER:

EMAIL:

CHILDREN & BIRTHDAYS:

FAVORITE MEMORY:

Reunion Guest Book

NAME:

BIRTHDAY: | ANNIVERSARY:

ADDRESS: ————

CONTACT NUMBER: | MOBILE NUMBER:

EMAIL:

CHILDREN & BIRTHDAYS:

FAVORITE MEMORY:

NAME:

BIRTHDAY: | ANNIVERSARY:

ADDRESS: ————

CONTACT NUMBER: | MOBILE NUMBER:

EMAIL:

CHILDREN & BIRTHDAYS:

FAVORITE MEMORY:

Reunion Guest Book

NAME:

BIRTHDAY: | ANNIVERSARY:

ADDRESS:

CONTACT NUMBER: | MOBILE NUMBER:

EMAIL:

CHILDREN & BIRTHDAYS:

FAVORITE MEMORY:

NAME:

BIRTHDAY: | ANNIVERSARY:

ADDRESS:

CONTACT NUMBER: | MOBILE NUMBER:

EMAIL:

CHILDREN & BIRTHDAYS:

FAVORITE MEMORY:

Reunion Guest Book

NAME:

BIRTHDAY: | ANNIVERSARY:

ADDRESS: ─────────

CONTACT NUMBER: | MOBILE NUMBER:

EMAIL:

CHILDREN & BIRTHDAYS:

FAVORITE MEMORY:

NAME:

BIRTHDAY: | ANNIVERSARY:

ADDRESS: ─────────

CONTACT NUMBER: | MOBILE NUMBER:

EMAIL:

CHILDREN & BIRTHDAYS:

FAVORITE MEMORY:

Reunion Guest Book

NAME:

BIRTHDAY: | ANNIVERSARY:

ADDRESS: ——————

CONTACT NUMBER: | MOBILE NUMBER:

EMAIL:

CHILDREN & BIRTHDAYS:

FAVORITE MEMORY:

NAME:

BIRTHDAY: | ANNIVERSARY:

ADDRESS: ——————

CONTACT NUMBER: | MOBILE NUMBER:

EMAIL:

CHILDREN & BIRTHDAYS:

FAVORITE MEMORY:

Reunion Guest Book

NAME:

BIRTHDAY: | ANNIVERSARY:

ADDRESS: —————————————————————————

CONTACT NUMBER: | MOBILE NUMBER:

EMAIL:

CHILDREN & BIRTHDAYS:

FAVORITE MEMORY:

NAME:

BIRTHDAY: | ANNIVERSARY:

ADDRESS: —————————————————————————

CONTACT NUMBER: | MOBILE NUMBER:

EMAIL:

CHILDREN & BIRTHDAYS:

FAVORITE MEMORY:

Reunion Guest Book

NAME:

BIRTHDAY: | ANNIVERSARY:

ADDRESS: ————

CONTACT NUMBER: | MOBILE NUMBER:

EMAIL:

CHILDREN & BIRTHDAYS:

FAVORITE MEMORY:

NAME:

BIRTHDAY: | ANNIVERSARY:

ADDRESS: ————

CONTACT NUMBER: | MOBILE NUMBER:

EMAIL:

CHILDREN & BIRTHDAYS:

FAVORITE MEMORY:

Reunion Guest Book

NAME:

BIRTHDAY: | ANNIVERSARY:

ADDRESS: —————————

CONTACT NUMBER: | MOBILE NUMBER:

EMAIL:

CHILDREN & BIRTHDAYS:

FAVORITE MEMORY:

NAME:

BIRTHDAY: | ANNIVERSARY:

ADDRESS: —————————

CONTACT NUMBER: | MOBILE NUMBER:

EMAIL:

CHILDREN & BIRTHDAYS:

FAVORITE MEMORY:

Reunion Guest Book

NAME:

BIRTHDAY: ANNIVERSARY:

ADDRESS: —————————————————

CONTACT NUMBER: MOBILE NUMBER:

EMAIL:

CHILDREN & BIRTHDAYS:

FAVORITE MEMORY:

NAME:

BIRTHDAY: ANNIVERSARY:

ADDRESS: —————————————————

CONTACT NUMBER: MOBILE NUMBER:

EMAIL:

CHILDREN & BIRTHDAYS:

FAVORITE MEMORY:

Reunion Guest Book

NAME:

BIRTHDAY: ANNIVERSARY:

ADDRESS: ————————————————

CONTACT NUMBER: MOBILE NUMBER:

EMAIL:

CHILDREN & BIRTHDAYS:

FAVORITE MEMORY:

NAME:

BIRTHDAY: ANNIVERSARY:

ADDRESS: ————————————————

CONTACT NUMBER: MOBILE NUMBER:

EMAIL:

CHILDREN & BIRTHDAYS:

FAVORITE MEMORY:

Reunion Guest Book

NAME:

BIRTHDAY: | ANNIVERSARY:

ADDRESS: —————————————————————————

CONTACT NUMBER: | MOBILE NUMBER:

EMAIL:

CHILDREN & BIRTHDAYS:

FAVORITE MEMORY:

NAME:

BIRTHDAY: | ANNIVERSARY:

ADDRESS: —————————————————————————

CONTACT NUMBER: | MOBILE NUMBER:

EMAIL:

CHILDREN & BIRTHDAYS:

FAVORITE MEMORY:

Reunion Guest Book

NAME:

BIRTHDAY: | ANNIVERSARY:

ADDRESS:

CONTACT NUMBER: | MOBILE NUMBER:

EMAIL:

CHILDREN & BIRTHDAYS:

FAVORITE MEMORY:

NAME:

BIRTHDAY: | ANNIVERSARY:

ADDRESS:

CONTACT NUMBER: | MOBILE NUMBER:

EMAIL:

CHILDREN & BIRTHDAYS:

FAVORITE MEMORY:

Reunion Guest Book

NAME:

BIRTHDAY: | ANNIVERSARY:

ADDRESS: ——————————————

CONTACT NUMBER: | MOBILE NUMBER:

EMAIL:

CHILDREN & BIRTHDAYS:

FAVORITE MEMORY:

NAME:

BIRTHDAY: | ANNIVERSARY:

ADDRESS: ——————————————

CONTACT NUMBER: | MOBILE NUMBER:

EMAIL:

CHILDREN & BIRTHDAYS:

FAVORITE MEMORY:

Reunion Guest Book

NAME:

BIRTHDAY: | ANNIVERSARY:

ADDRESS:

CONTACT NUMBER: | MOBILE NUMBER:

EMAIL:

CHILDREN & BIRTHDAYS:

FAVORITE MEMORY:

NAME:

BIRTHDAY: | ANNIVERSARY:

ADDRESS:

CONTACT NUMBER: | MOBILE NUMBER:

EMAIL:

CHILDREN & BIRTHDAYS:

FAVORITE MEMORY:

Reunion Guest Book

NAME:

BIRTHDAY: | ANNIVERSARY:

ADDRESS:

CONTACT NUMBER: | MOBILE NUMBER:

EMAIL:

CHILDREN & BIRTHDAYS:

FAVORITE MEMORY:

NAME:

BIRTHDAY: | ANNIVERSARY:

ADDRESS:

CONTACT NUMBER: | MOBILE NUMBER:

EMAIL:

CHILDREN & BIRTHDAYS:

FAVORITE MEMORY:

Reunion Guest Book

NAME:

BIRTHDAY: | ANNIVERSARY:

ADDRESS: —

CONTACT NUMBER: | MOBILE NUMBER:

EMAIL:

CHILDREN & BIRTHDAYS:

FAVORITE MEMORY:

NAME:

BIRTHDAY: | ANNIVERSARY:

ADDRESS: —

CONTACT NUMBER: | MOBILE NUMBER:

EMAIL:

CHILDREN & BIRTHDAYS:

FAVORITE MEMORY:

Reunion Guest Book

NAME:

BIRTHDAY: ANNIVERSARY:

ADDRESS: ———————————————————

CONTACT NUMBER: MOBILE NUMBER:

EMAIL:

CHILDREN & BIRTHDAYS:

FAVORITE MEMORY:

NAME:

BIRTHDAY: ANNIVERSARY:

ADDRESS: ———————————————————

CONTACT NUMBER: MOBILE NUMBER:

EMAIL:

CHILDREN & BIRTHDAYS:

FAVORITE MEMORY:

Reunion Guest Book

NAME:

BIRTHDAY: | ANNIVERSARY:

ADDRESS:

CONTACT NUMBER: | MOBILE NUMBER:

EMAIL:

CHILDREN & BIRTHDAYS:

FAVORITE MEMORY:

NAME:

BIRTHDAY: | ANNIVERSARY:

ADDRESS:

CONTACT NUMBER: | MOBILE NUMBER:

EMAIL:

CHILDREN & BIRTHDAYS:

FAVORITE MEMORY:

Reunion Guest Book

NAME:

BIRTHDAY: | ANNIVERSARY:

ADDRESS: ———————————————

CONTACT NUMBER: | MOBILE NUMBER:

EMAIL:

CHILDREN & BIRTHDAYS:

FAVORITE MEMORY:

NAME:

BIRTHDAY: | ANNIVERSARY:

ADDRESS: ———————————————

CONTACT NUMBER: | MOBILE NUMBER:

EMAIL:

CHILDREN & BIRTHDAYS:

FAVORITE MEMORY:

Reunion Guest Book

NAME:

BIRTHDAY: | ANNIVERSARY:

ADDRESS: —————————

CONTACT NUMBER: | MOBILE NUMBER:

EMAIL:

CHILDREN & BIRTHDAYS:

FAVORITE MEMORY:

NAME:

BIRTHDAY: | ANNIVERSARY:

ADDRESS: —————————

CONTACT NUMBER: | MOBILE NUMBER:

EMAIL:

CHILDREN & BIRTHDAYS:

FAVORITE MEMORY:

Reunion Guest Book

NAME:

BIRTHDAY: | ANNIVERSARY:

ADDRESS: —————————————————————

CONTACT NUMBER: | MOBILE NUMBER:

EMAIL:

CHILDREN & BIRTHDAYS:

FAVORITE MEMORY:

NAME:

BIRTHDAY: | ANNIVERSARY:

ADDRESS: —————————————————————

CONTACT NUMBER: | MOBILE NUMBER:

EMAIL:

CHILDREN & BIRTHDAYS:

FAVORITE MEMORY:

Reunion Guest Book

NAME:

BIRTHDAY: | ANNIVERSARY:

ADDRESS: ————————————————

CONTACT NUMBER: | MOBILE NUMBER:

EMAIL:

CHILDREN & BIRTHDAYS:

FAVORITE MEMORY:

NAME:

BIRTHDAY: | ANNIVERSARY:

ADDRESS: ————————————————

CONTACT NUMBER: | MOBILE NUMBER:

EMAIL:

CHILDREN & BIRTHDAYS:

FAVORITE MEMORY:

Reunion Guest Book

NAME:

BIRTHDAY: | ANNIVERSARY:

ADDRESS: ———————————————————

CONTACT NUMBER: | MOBILE NUMBER:

EMAIL:

CHILDREN & BIRTHDAYS:

FAVORITE MEMORY:

NAME:

BIRTHDAY: | ANNIVERSARY:

ADDRESS: ———————————————————

CONTACT NUMBER: | MOBILE NUMBER:

EMAIL:

CHILDREN & BIRTHDAYS:

FAVORITE MEMORY:

Reunion Guest Book

NAME:

BIRTHDAY: | ANNIVERSARY:

ADDRESS: —————————————

CONTACT NUMBER: | MOBILE NUMBER:

EMAIL:

CHILDREN & BIRTHDAYS:

FAVORITE MEMORY:

NAME:

BIRTHDAY: | ANNIVERSARY:

ADDRESS: —————————————

CONTACT NUMBER: | MOBILE NUMBER:

EMAIL:

CHILDREN & BIRTHDAYS:

FAVORITE MEMORY:

Reunion Guest Book

NAME:

BIRTHDAY: | ANNIVERSARY:

ADDRESS: —————————————

CONTACT NUMBER: | MOBILE NUMBER:

EMAIL:

CHILDREN & BIRTHDAYS:

FAVORITE MEMORY:

NAME:

BIRTHDAY: | ANNIVERSARY:

ADDRESS: —————————————

CONTACT NUMBER: | MOBILE NUMBER:

EMAIL:

CHILDREN & BIRTHDAYS:

FAVORITE MEMORY:

Reunion Guest Book

NAME:

BIRTHDAY: | ANNIVERSARY:

ADDRESS: ————

CONTACT NUMBER: | MOBILE NUMBER:

EMAIL:

CHILDREN & BIRTHDAYS:

FAVORITE MEMORY:

NAME:

BIRTHDAY: | ANNIVERSARY:

ADDRESS: ————

CONTACT NUMBER: | MOBILE NUMBER:

EMAIL:

CHILDREN & BIRTHDAYS:

FAVORITE MEMORY:

Reunion Guest Book

NAME:

BIRTHDAY: | ANNIVERSARY:

ADDRESS:

CONTACT NUMBER: | MOBILE NUMBER:

EMAIL:

CHILDREN & BIRTHDAYS:

FAVORITE MEMORY:

NAME:

BIRTHDAY: | ANNIVERSARY:

ADDRESS:

CONTACT NUMBER: | MOBILE NUMBER:

EMAIL:

CHILDREN & BIRTHDAYS:

FAVORITE MEMORY:

Reunion Guest Book

NAME:

BIRTHDAY: | ANNIVERSARY:

ADDRESS:

CONTACT NUMBER: | MOBILE NUMBER:

EMAIL:

CHILDREN & BIRTHDAYS:

FAVORITE MEMORY:

NAME:

BIRTHDAY: | ANNIVERSARY:

ADDRESS:

CONTACT NUMBER: | MOBILE NUMBER:

EMAIL:

CHILDREN & BIRTHDAYS:

FAVORITE MEMORY:

Reunion Guest Book

NAME:

BIRTHDAY: | ANNIVERSARY:

ADDRESS: ———

CONTACT NUMBER: | MOBILE NUMBER:

EMAIL:

CHILDREN & BIRTHDAYS:

FAVORITE MEMORY:

NAME:

BIRTHDAY: | ANNIVERSARY:

ADDRESS: ———

CONTACT NUMBER: | MOBILE NUMBER:

EMAIL:

CHILDREN & BIRTHDAYS:

FAVORITE MEMORY:

Reunion Guest Book

NAME:

BIRTHDAY: | ANNIVERSARY:

ADDRESS: —

CONTACT NUMBER: | MOBILE NUMBER:

EMAIL:

CHILDREN & BIRTHDAYS:

FAVORITE MEMORY:

NAME:

BIRTHDAY: | ANNIVERSARY:

ADDRESS: —

CONTACT NUMBER: | MOBILE NUMBER:

EMAIL:

CHILDREN & BIRTHDAYS:

FAVORITE MEMORY:

Reunion Guest Book

NAME:

BIRTHDAY: | ANNIVERSARY:

ADDRESS: ————————————————

CONTACT NUMBER: | MOBILE NUMBER:

EMAIL:

CHILDREN & BIRTHDAYS:

FAVORITE MEMORY:

NAME:

BIRTHDAY: | ANNIVERSARY:

ADDRESS: ————————————————

CONTACT NUMBER: | MOBILE NUMBER:

EMAIL:

CHILDREN & BIRTHDAYS:

FAVORITE MEMORY:

Reunion Guest Book

NAME:

BIRTHDAY: | ANNIVERSARY:

ADDRESS: —————————————————————————

CONTACT NUMBER: | MOBILE NUMBER:

EMAIL:

CHILDREN & BIRTHDAYS:

FAVORITE MEMORY:

NAME:

BIRTHDAY: | ANNIVERSARY:

ADDRESS: —————————————————————————

CONTACT NUMBER: | MOBILE NUMBER:

EMAIL:

CHILDREN & BIRTHDAYS:

FAVORITE MEMORY:

Reunion Guest Book

NAME:

BIRTHDAY: | ANNIVERSARY:

ADDRESS:

CONTACT NUMBER: | MOBILE NUMBER:

EMAIL:

CHILDREN & BIRTHDAYS:

FAVORITE MEMORY:

NAME:

BIRTHDAY: | ANNIVERSARY:

ADDRESS:

CONTACT NUMBER: | MOBILE NUMBER:

EMAIL:

CHILDREN & BIRTHDAYS:

FAVORITE MEMORY:

Reunion Guest Book

NAME:

BIRTHDAY: ANNIVERSARY:

ADDRESS: —————————————————

CONTACT NUMBER: MOBILE NUMBER:

EMAIL:

CHILDREN & BIRTHDAYS:

FAVORITE MEMORY:

NAME:

BIRTHDAY: ANNIVERSARY:

ADDRESS: —————————————————

CONTACT NUMBER: MOBILE NUMBER:

EMAIL:

CHILDREN & BIRTHDAYS:

FAVORITE MEMORY:

Reunion Guest Book

NAME:

BIRTHDAY: | ANNIVERSARY:

ADDRESS:

CONTACT NUMBER: | MOBILE NUMBER:

EMAIL:

CHILDREN & BIRTHDAYS:

FAVORITE MEMORY:

NAME:

BIRTHDAY: | ANNIVERSARY:

ADDRESS:

CONTACT NUMBER: | MOBILE NUMBER:

EMAIL:

CHILDREN & BIRTHDAYS:

FAVORITE MEMORY:

Reunion Guest Book

NAME:

BIRTHDAY: | ANNIVERSARY:

ADDRESS:

CONTACT NUMBER: | MOBILE NUMBER:

EMAIL:

CHILDREN & BIRTHDAYS:

FAVORITE MEMORY:

NAME:

BIRTHDAY: | ANNIVERSARY:

ADDRESS:

CONTACT NUMBER: | MOBILE NUMBER:

EMAIL:

CHILDREN & BIRTHDAYS:

FAVORITE MEMORY:

Reunion Guest Book

NAME:

BIRTHDAY: ANNIVERSARY:

ADDRESS: ──────────

CONTACT NUMBER: MOBILE NUMBER:

EMAIL:

CHILDREN & BIRTHDAYS:

FAVORITE MEMORY:

NAME:

BIRTHDAY: ANNIVERSARY:

ADDRESS: ──────────

CONTACT NUMBER: MOBILE NUMBER:

EMAIL:

CHILDREN & BIRTHDAYS:

FAVORITE MEMORY:

Reunion Guest Book

NAME:

BIRTHDAY: | ANNIVERSARY:

ADDRESS: —————————————————————

CONTACT NUMBER: | MOBILE NUMBER:

EMAIL:

CHILDREN & BIRTHDAYS:

FAVORITE MEMORY:

NAME:

BIRTHDAY: | ANNIVERSARY:

ADDRESS: —————————————————————

CONTACT NUMBER: | MOBILE NUMBER:

EMAIL:

CHILDREN & BIRTHDAYS:

FAVORITE MEMORY:

Reunion Guest Book

NAME:

BIRTHDAY: ANNIVERSARY:

ADDRESS:

CONTACT NUMBER: MOBILE NUMBER:

EMAIL:

CHILDREN & BIRTHDAYS:

FAVORITE MEMORY:

NAME:

BIRTHDAY: ANNIVERSARY:

ADDRESS:

CONTACT NUMBER: MOBILE NUMBER:

EMAIL:

CHILDREN & BIRTHDAYS:

FAVORITE MEMORY:

Reunion Guest Book

NAME:

BIRTHDAY: | ANNIVERSARY:

ADDRESS: ——————————————

CONTACT NUMBER: | MOBILE NUMBER:

EMAIL:

CHILDREN & BIRTHDAYS:

FAVORITE MEMORY:

NAME:

BIRTHDAY: | ANNIVERSARY:

ADDRESS: ——————————————

CONTACT NUMBER: | MOBILE NUMBER:

EMAIL:

CHILDREN & BIRTHDAYS:

FAVORITE MEMORY:

Reunion Guest Book

NAME:

BIRTHDAY: | ANNIVERSARY:

ADDRESS:

CONTACT NUMBER: | MOBILE NUMBER:

EMAIL:

CHILDREN & BIRTHDAYS:

FAVORITE MEMORY:

NAME:

BIRTHDAY: | ANNIVERSARY:

ADDRESS:

CONTACT NUMBER: | MOBILE NUMBER:

EMAIL:

CHILDREN & BIRTHDAYS:

FAVORITE MEMORY:

Reunion Guest Book

NAME:

BIRTHDAY: | ANNIVERSARY:

ADDRESS: ——————————————

CONTACT NUMBER: | MOBILE NUMBER:

EMAIL:

CHILDREN & BIRTHDAYS:

FAVORITE MEMORY:

NAME:

BIRTHDAY: | ANNIVERSARY:

ADDRESS: ——————————————

CONTACT NUMBER: | MOBILE NUMBER:

EMAIL:

CHILDREN & BIRTHDAYS:

FAVORITE MEMORY:

Reunion Guest Book

NAME:

BIRTHDAY:	ANNIVERSARY:

ADDRESS: —————————————————————

CONTACT NUMBER:	MOBILE NUMBER:

EMAIL:

CHILDREN & BIRTHDAYS:

FAVORITE MEMORY:

NAME:

BIRTHDAY:	ANNIVERSARY:

ADDRESS: —————————————————————

CONTACT NUMBER:	MOBILE NUMBER:

EMAIL:

CHILDREN & BIRTHDAYS:

FAVORITE MEMORY:

Reunion Guest Book

NAME:

BIRTHDAY: | ANNIVERSARY:

ADDRESS:

CONTACT NUMBER: | MOBILE NUMBER:

EMAIL:

CHILDREN & BIRTHDAYS:

FAVORITE MEMORY:

NAME:

BIRTHDAY: | ANNIVERSARY:

ADDRESS:

CONTACT NUMBER: | MOBILE NUMBER:

EMAIL:

CHILDREN & BIRTHDAYS:

FAVORITE MEMORY:

Reunion Guest Book

NAME:

| BIRTHDAY: | ANNIVERSARY: |

ADDRESS: ————————————————

| CONTACT NUMBER: | MOBILE NUMBER: |

EMAIL:

CHILDREN & BIRTHDAYS:

FAVORITE MEMORY:

NAME:

| BIRTHDAY: | ANNIVERSARY: |

ADDRESS: ————————————————

| CONTACT NUMBER: | MOBILE NUMBER: |

EMAIL:

CHILDREN & BIRTHDAYS:

FAVORITE MEMORY:

Reunion Guest Book

NAME:

BIRTHDAY: ANNIVERSARY:

ADDRESS: ——————————————————————

CONTACT NUMBER: MOBILE NUMBER:

EMAIL:

CHILDREN & BIRTHDAYS:

FAVORITE MEMORY:

NAME:

BIRTHDAY: ANNIVERSARY:

ADDRESS: ——————————————————————

CONTACT NUMBER: MOBILE NUMBER:

EMAIL:

CHILDREN & BIRTHDAYS:

FAVORITE MEMORY:

Reunion Guest Book

NAME:

BIRTHDAY: | ANNIVERSARY:

ADDRESS:

CONTACT NUMBER: | MOBILE NUMBER:

EMAIL:

CHILDREN & BIRTHDAYS:

FAVORITE MEMORY:

NAME:

BIRTHDAY: | ANNIVERSARY:

ADDRESS:

CONTACT NUMBER: | MOBILE NUMBER:

EMAIL:

CHILDREN & BIRTHDAYS:

FAVORITE MEMORY:

Reunion Guest Book

NAME:

BIRTHDAY: ANNIVERSARY:

ADDRESS: ————————————————————

CONTACT NUMBER: MOBILE NUMBER:

EMAIL:

CHILDREN & BIRTHDAYS:

FAVORITE MEMORY:

NAME:

BIRTHDAY: ANNIVERSARY:

ADDRESS: ————————————————————

CONTACT NUMBER: MOBILE NUMBER:

EMAIL:

CHILDREN & BIRTHDAYS:

FAVORITE MEMORY:

Reunion Guest Book

NAME:

BIRTHDAY: | ANNIVERSARY:

ADDRESS:

CONTACT NUMBER: | MOBILE NUMBER:

EMAIL:

CHILDREN & BIRTHDAYS:

FAVORITE MEMORY:

NAME:

BIRTHDAY: | ANNIVERSARY:

ADDRESS:

CONTACT NUMBER: | MOBILE NUMBER:

EMAIL:

CHILDREN & BIRTHDAYS:

FAVORITE MEMORY:

Reunion Guest Book

NAME:

BIRTHDAY: | ANNIVERSARY:

ADDRESS: ———————————————

CONTACT NUMBER: | MOBILE NUMBER:

EMAIL:

CHILDREN & BIRTHDAYS:

FAVORITE MEMORY:

NAME:

BIRTHDAY: | ANNIVERSARY:

ADDRESS: ———————————————

CONTACT NUMBER: | MOBILE NUMBER:

EMAIL:

CHILDREN & BIRTHDAYS:

FAVORITE MEMORY:

Reunion Guest Book

NAME:

BIRTHDAY: | ANNIVERSARY:

ADDRESS: ——————————

CONTACT NUMBER: | MOBILE NUMBER:

EMAIL:

CHILDREN & BIRTHDAYS:

FAVORITE MEMORY:

NAME:

BIRTHDAY: | ANNIVERSARY:

ADDRESS: ——————————

CONTACT NUMBER: | MOBILE NUMBER:

EMAIL:

CHILDREN & BIRTHDAYS:

FAVORITE MEMORY:

Reunion Guest Book

NAME:

BIRTHDAY:

ANNIVERSARY:

ADDRESS: ———————————————

CONTACT NUMBER:

MOBILE NUMBER:

EMAIL:

CHILDREN & BIRTHDAYS:

FAVORITE MEMORY:

NAME:

BIRTHDAY:

ANNIVERSARY:

ADDRESS: ———————————————

CONTACT NUMBER:

MOBILE NUMBER:

EMAIL:

CHILDREN & BIRTHDAYS:

FAVORITE MEMORY:

Reunion Guest Book

NAME:

BIRTHDAY: | ANNIVERSARY:

ADDRESS: ———————————————

CONTACT NUMBER: | MOBILE NUMBER:

EMAIL:

CHILDREN & BIRTHDAYS:

FAVORITE MEMORY:

NAME:

BIRTHDAY: | ANNIVERSARY:

ADDRESS: ———————————————

CONTACT NUMBER: | MOBILE NUMBER:

EMAIL:

CHILDREN & BIRTHDAYS:

FAVORITE MEMORY:

Reunion Guest Book

NAME:

BIRTHDAY: | ANNIVERSARY:

ADDRESS:

CONTACT NUMBER: | MOBILE NUMBER:

EMAIL:

CHILDREN & BIRTHDAYS:

FAVORITE MEMORY:

NAME:

BIRTHDAY: | ANNIVERSARY:

ADDRESS:

CONTACT NUMBER: | MOBILE NUMBER:

EMAIL:

CHILDREN & BIRTHDAYS:

FAVORITE MEMORY:

Reunion Guest Book

NAME:

BIRTHDAY: | ANNIVERSARY:

ADDRESS: ——————————————————————

CONTACT NUMBER: | MOBILE NUMBER:

EMAIL:

CHILDREN & BIRTHDAYS:

FAVORITE MEMORY:

NAME:

BIRTHDAY: | ANNIVERSARY:

ADDRESS: ——————————————————————

CONTACT NUMBER: | MOBILE NUMBER:

EMAIL:

CHILDREN & BIRTHDAYS:

FAVORITE MEMORY:

Reunion Guest Book

NAME:

BIRTHDAY: | ANNIVERSARY:

ADDRESS: —————

CONTACT NUMBER: | MOBILE NUMBER:

EMAIL:

CHILDREN & BIRTHDAYS:

FAVORITE MEMORY:

NAME:

BIRTHDAY: | ANNIVERSARY:

ADDRESS: —————

CONTACT NUMBER: | MOBILE NUMBER:

EMAIL:

CHILDREN & BIRTHDAYS:

FAVORITE MEMORY:

Reunion Guest Book

NAME:

BIRTHDAY:

ANNIVERSARY:

ADDRESS: ————————————————————

CONTACT NUMBER:

MOBILE NUMBER:

EMAIL:

CHILDREN & BIRTHDAYS:

FAVORITE MEMORY:

NAME:

BIRTHDAY:

ANNIVERSARY:

ADDRESS: ————————————————————

CONTACT NUMBER:

MOBILE NUMBER:

EMAIL:

CHILDREN & BIRTHDAYS:

FAVORITE MEMORY:

Reunion Guest Book

NAME:

BIRTHDAY: ANNIVERSARY:

ADDRESS: —————————————————————

CONTACT NUMBER: MOBILE NUMBER:

EMAIL:

CHILDREN & BIRTHDAYS:

FAVORITE MEMORY:

NAME:

BIRTHDAY: ANNIVERSARY:

ADDRESS: —————————————————————

CONTACT NUMBER: MOBILE NUMBER:

EMAIL:

CHILDREN & BIRTHDAYS:

FAVORITE MEMORY:

Reunion Guest Book

NAME:

BIRTHDAY: | ANNIVERSARY:

ADDRESS: ——————

CONTACT NUMBER: | MOBILE NUMBER:

EMAIL:

CHILDREN & BIRTHDAYS:

FAVORITE MEMORY:

NAME:

BIRTHDAY: | ANNIVERSARY:

ADDRESS: ——————

CONTACT NUMBER: | MOBILE NUMBER:

EMAIL:

CHILDREN & BIRTHDAYS:

FAVORITE MEMORY:

Reunion Guest Book

NAME:

BIRTHDAY: ANNIVERSARY:

ADDRESS: ——————————————————

CONTACT NUMBER: MOBILE NUMBER:

EMAIL:

CHILDREN & BIRTHDAYS:

FAVORITE MEMORY:

NAME:

BIRTHDAY: ANNIVERSARY:

ADDRESS: ——————————————————

CONTACT NUMBER: MOBILE NUMBER:

EMAIL:

CHILDREN & BIRTHDAYS:

FAVORITE MEMORY:

Reunion Guest Book

NAME:

BIRTHDAY: | ANNIVERSARY:

ADDRESS: —————————————————————

CONTACT NUMBER: | MOBILE NUMBER:

EMAIL:

CHILDREN & BIRTHDAYS:

FAVORITE MEMORY:

NAME:

BIRTHDAY: | ANNIVERSARY:

ADDRESS: —————————————————————

CONTACT NUMBER: | MOBILE NUMBER:

EMAIL:

CHILDREN & BIRTHDAYS:

FAVORITE MEMORY:

Reunion Guest Book

NAME:

BIRTHDAY:

ANNIVERSARY:

ADDRESS: ———————————————————

CONTACT NUMBER:

MOBILE NUMBER:

EMAIL:

CHILDREN & BIRTHDAYS:

FAVORITE MEMORY:

NAME:

BIRTHDAY:

ANNIVERSARY:

ADDRESS: ———————————————————

CONTACT NUMBER:

MOBILE NUMBER:

EMAIL:

CHILDREN & BIRTHDAYS:

FAVORITE MEMORY:

Reunion Guest Book

NAME:

BIRTHDAY:	ANNIVERSARY:

ADDRESS: —————————————————————

CONTACT NUMBER:	MOBILE NUMBER:

EMAIL:

CHILDREN & BIRTHDAYS:

FAVORITE MEMORY:

NAME:

BIRTHDAY:	ANNIVERSARY:

ADDRESS: —————————————————————

CONTACT NUMBER:	MOBILE NUMBER:

EMAIL:

CHILDREN & BIRTHDAYS:

FAVORITE MEMORY:

Reunion Guest Book

NAME:

BIRTHDAY: | ANNIVERSARY:

ADDRESS: ———————————————

CONTACT NUMBER: | MOBILE NUMBER:

EMAIL:

CHILDREN & BIRTHDAYS:

FAVORITE MEMORY:

NAME:

BIRTHDAY: | ANNIVERSARY:

ADDRESS: ———————————————

CONTACT NUMBER: | MOBILE NUMBER:

EMAIL:

CHILDREN & BIRTHDAYS:

FAVORITE MEMORY:

Reunion Guest Book

NAME:

BIRTHDAY: ANNIVERSARY:

ADDRESS: ————————————————————

CONTACT NUMBER: MOBILE NUMBER:

EMAIL:

CHILDREN & BIRTHDAYS:

FAVORITE MEMORY:

NAME:

BIRTHDAY: ANNIVERSARY:

ADDRESS: ————————————————————

CONTACT NUMBER: MOBILE NUMBER:

EMAIL:

CHILDREN & BIRTHDAYS:

FAVORITE MEMORY:

Reunion Guest Book

NAME:

BIRTHDAY:

ANNIVERSARY:

ADDRESS: —————————————————————

CONTACT NUMBER:

MOBILE NUMBER:

EMAIL:

CHILDREN & BIRTHDAYS:

FAVORITE MEMORY:

NAME:

BIRTHDAY:

ANNIVERSARY:

ADDRESS: —————————————————————

CONTACT NUMBER:

MOBILE NUMBER:

EMAIL:

CHILDREN & BIRTHDAYS:

FAVORITE MEMORY:

Notes

Notes

Notes

Made in the USA
Monee, IL
13 December 2021